Meet Me *Under* The Maple Tree

Ceneca Van Tassell-Luto

Illustrated By Sean Winburn

AuthorHouse™
1663 Liberty Drive
Bloomington, IN 47403
www.authorhouse.com
Phone: 1 (800) 839-8640

Published by AuthorHouse 04/22/2019

ISBN: 978-1-7283-0878-4 (sc)

Library of Congress Control Number: 2019904664

Print information available on the last page.

authorHOUSE®

Dedication

⤜⤛⤜

I dedicate this book to my sister, Cathy. I wouldn't have
the wonderful memories of our visits with our grandparents
if it wasn't for her. We have been through so much together
throughout our lives. I am so blessed to have been given such a
wonderful sister. I love you, Cathy!

"Are we almost there?," chirped Katy anxiously from the back seat of mom's old sedan. Katy Sunbeam was so excited to see her grandparents.

The old maple tree, in the sleepy little town of Porterville, was the designated meeting place. Katy's suitcase had been packed for days. She was as excited as a pig in mud to get to her grandparents' farm.

School was out for the summer which meant a fun week for Katy at their farm. She loved being at the farm. The big white farmhouse sat on 50 acres of land. Katy and her sister, Cathy, always looked forward to their summer visits.

Katy spotted the ol' brown truck resting under the maple tree. She shrieked so loudly she startled her mom.

"Katy Sunbeam, I know you're excited, but do you have to be so loud?," her mom grumbled.

Grandpa and Grandma were there to meet Katy and Cathy. The girls kissed their mom good-bye. They promised to help their grandparents and to take a bath each night. (Out on the farm, you can get quite dirty.)

As the ol' brown truck pulled away, Katy and Cathy waved to their mom and blew her kisses out the back window, as she headed down the road in the opposite direction.

The ol' brown truck bumped along the gravel road towards the white farmhouse. The tink-tonk, tink-tonk of the blinker was a signal to Katy and Cathy that the ol' brown truck was about to pull into the driveway. "We're here!," they joyously shouted.

The doors flew open and out they jumped. They grabbed their suitcases, raced into the house, sprinted up the stairs, unpacked their bags, and flopped on the old feather bed, excited to plan their week-long adventure at the farm.

MONDAY- Katy and Cathy awoke to the smell of bacon frying in the kitchen and the stairs creaking below as their grandpa ambled up the staircase to wake them. He stood at the top of the steps and bellowed, "Get up and wash your sassy faces. Breakfast is ready!"

The girls hopped out of bed. They jumped on the banister and gingerly slid all the way down.

After a yummy country breakfast, Katy and Cathy headed for the gravel road in front of the farmhouse. They plopped down in the middle of the road and started searching for Indian beads, which are rocks with a hole in the middle. Each time the girls visited, they would search for Indian beads and add the newly found beads to their Indian bead necklace that their grandma had helped them start.

While sitting in the middle of the road, both girls would get very dirty. Katy Sunbeam loved getting dirty because it was so much fun getting cleaned up.

Katy and Cathy pumped icy cold water from the well into buckets and carefully filled up the old horse trough. The girls would playfully splash around in the trough for hours.

TUESDAY- "Get up and wash your sassy faces. It's Tuesday, so that means laundry day!," bellowed Grandpa from the top of the stairs. Down the banister they slid going round and round.

Out in the backyard, their grandma had set up the old washer. Both girls donned their aprons and were ready to report for laundry duty.

Katy Sunbeam loved her grandma's old-fashioned washing machine. Once again, the girls had to pump icy cold water from the well to fill up the washer. The clothes churned round and round and up and down as the water splashed in the big ol' steel tank.

The girls enjoyed helping their grandma wring out the water from the clothes. Katy fed the clothes through the wringer while Cathy turned the big wooden handle. There wasn't a drop of water left in the clothes by the time the girls were finished.

When all of the clothes were washed and wrung out, it was time to hang them on the clothesline.

That's when the aprons came in handy. The girls had wooden clothespins in their apron pockets.

Believe it or not, there is an art to hanging up clothes.

Their grandma had three long lines where the clothes were to be hung. Shirts and pants were pinned to the line upside down. All of the clothes were hooked together like cars on a train.

Katy loved the smell of her sheets each time she crawled into bed. The crisp sheets smelled as fresh as an ocean breeze. As she fell asleep, she thought . . . there's nothing better than snuggling up in grandma's sheets after they've hung outside to dry.

WEDNESDAY- "Get up and wash your sassy faces," came the bellow from atop the stairs.

It was still pitch black outside. The girls hadn't even heard the rooster crow yet. The red digits on the clock read 5:00 a.m. Katy and Cathy knew what was in store for them today. This was the day to help Grandpa take the pigs to market! Soo-wee!

A quick breakfast was gulped down and then the girls headed for the truck.

The pigs weren't kept near the farmhouse. That was a good thing! Have you ever smelled pigs? Katy's grandpa kept the pigs on his farmland about five miles from their white farmhouse.

The girls knew they were getting close because of the pungent aroma in the air. Katy Sunbeam hopped out of the ol' truck and opened the latch on the gate so her grandpa could drive the ol' brown truck into the field. She latched the gate and hopped on the back of the tailgate to ride through the field.

Soo-wee! Here pig, pig, pig! Katy and Cathy giggled as their grandpa called the pigs. When they stopped giggling, they chimed in and helped their grandpa call the pigs.

Six pigs at a time were loaded into the ol' brown truck. Three trips were made to market that day. Boy, did that ol' truck get dirty. Katy and Cathy rode in the cab of the truck and tried to guess the weight of the pigs.

The girl's great-grandparents lived on the way to the market. Their grandpa was good to his pigs and would stop at their great-grandparents' house, so the girls could hop out and pump two buckets of water to throw on the pigs. You see, pigs don't sweat. They have to be moved early in the morning when it is cool outside. On market days, you leave before the rooster crows.

THURSDAY- The stairs creaked so the girls put the covers over their heads to trick their grandpa into thinking they were still asleep. It worked. The creaking stopped and then all of a sudden they heard, "Get up and wash your sassy faces. Breakfast is ready!"

Down the banister they twirled, going round and round.

Katy and Cathy gobbled down their good ol' country breakfast and skipped out to the ol' brown truck. Today was the day to help Grandpa build some hog houses.

The dust from the old country roads swirled like funnel clouds as the ol' brown truck made its way to the fields where the pigs roamed.

The pigs came a runnin' when they spotted Grandpa's truck. Katy and Cathy scooped out some corn from the back of the truck. Oink-oink came the thank you's from the pigs.

Did you know that you can ride a pig? You sure can! The trick is having lots of corn. Katy's and Cathy's mom was an awesome pig rider. She taught the girls at an early age how to ride pigs. Are you ready to learn? Listen carefully.

The girls knew the steps well. First, you have to spot the pig that is most interested in their corn. Sneak up behind it and grab hold of its tail. As you do that, hoist yourself up on the pig's back and grab their ears ... gently. Yee-haa! The ride is rough, but hang on tight until they bounce you off.

When you finally fall off, you better hop up and run back to the truck as fast as you can because the pig will chase you. And that's just what Katy and Cathy did.

After the pigs settled down from their wild adventure, Katy Sunbeam and Cathy thought it was safe to leave the back of the truck and scurry over to where their grandpa was building the hog houses.

The girls' grandpa was very good to his momma pigs. He always built hog houses for them to raise their families each year.

The houses were built in an A-frame style. Katy and Cathy helped hold the wood while their grandpa pounded in the nails. Bang! Bang! Bang!

After the frame was built, Grandpa nailed sheets of tin onto the boards. Bang! Bang! Bang! Each house took about two hours to build.

Grandpa called it a day when he had completed three hog houses. The ol' brown truck churned up dust as it ambled on back to the white farmhouse.

FRIDAY- Katy and Cathy listened to the early sounds of morning as they laid in bed trying to wake up. The birds were chirp, chirp, chirping. The leaves were rustling against the windows in the cool morning breeze. The stairs were creak, creak, creaking! The girls knew just what that meant . . . Grandpa was coming up the steps to wake them up. They covered their heads and listened.

"Get up and wash your sassy faces. The morning's almost over. Grandma has breakfast ready for you!," their grandpa bellowed loudly.

Down the banister they twirled going round and round.

Katy's favorite breakfast was waiting for her. A big bowl of rice. Katy Sunbeam loved her grandma's rice. She scooped some of the steaming rice into a bowl. She sprinkled some sugar on it, a little cinnamon, a dollop of butter, and then drenched it with milk. Katy loved her rice fixed this way. Yum, yum!

The girls were anxious to get outside and try out the new wooden tree swing their grandpa had hung up for them.

The old oak tree in the backyard had a branch perfect for the swing.

While their grandma washed the breakfast dishes, she watched from the kitchen window as the sisters played on the swing. She loved to hear them giggle.

The rope swing was great fun for Katy and Cathy. They took turns pushing each other. With each push, the ropes on the swing creaked as the girls went higher and higher, hoping to touch the bright green leaves on the tippy top branches of the old oak tree.

SATURDAY- "Get up and wash your sassy faces," Grandpa bellowed once again. Katy and Cathy were hoping to sleep in today. After all, it was Saturday.

They bounded out of bed and headed for the banister. The smell of breakfast tickled their noses. Breakfast was gobbled down because they heard the ol' John Deere outside purr to life. Katy and Cathy knew what that meant . . . a ride on the tractor.

Grandpa was in the big, yellow seat waiting for the girls to hop on board. The tire covers, over each wheel, served wonderfully as seats for Katy and Cathy.

Grandpa put the ol' John Deere into gear while the girls held on tightly. As they chugged down the gravel road, the dust kicked up and looked like a swarm of bees were following them.

About a mile down the road, just out of Grandma's sight, Katy crawled onto her grandpa's lap and anxiously grabbed the black cushioned steering wheel. Grandpa couldn't see it, but Katy had a huge grin on her little freckled face as her blonde pigtails blew carelessly in the wind.

Two miles down the dusty road, the girls traded places. It was Cathy's turn to drive now. She shared the same grin as Katy.

It was always fun with grandpa out on the ol' John Deere.

SUNDAY- Katy and Cathy whispered and reminisced as they laid in bed, thinking about their fun-filled, action-packed, non-stop adventures on the farm.

The stairs started to creak. The girls quickly put the sheets over their heads and laid ever so quietly, just waiting for that bellow. Wait for it . . . wait for it. There it was, right on cue. "Girls, get up and wash your sassy faces. Breakfast is ready."

They jumped out of bed and hopped on the banister like cowboys mounting their horses. Down they went, knowing this was the last morning to slide down the beloved banister for a while. Today they were to meet their mom under the old maple tree.

After breakfast, the girls helped their grandma wash and dry the dishes, and laughed about their week together.

When the last dish was dried and put away, Grandma told the girls it was time to get ready for church.

The singing was the best part of church. The girls looked forward to the music at the little country church, on the side of the road. Their grandpa was a wonderful singer, but boy was he loud. It was Mildred that made the singing so interesting. She was as off-key as Grandpa was loud. The girls struggled to not laugh during each song.

Katy's grandpa was the Sunday School teacher. He always delivered a heartfelt lesson at the little country church on the side of the road.

Sunday dinner was Grandma's specialty. The dishes on the table were filled with fried chicken, homemade noodles, mashed potatoes, and white gravy made from the fried chicken grease. You haven't lived 'till you've eaten Grandma's white gravy. Yum!

After Grandpa's blessing of the food, the girls scooped up the mashed potatoes and gravy like there was no tomorrow. Their favorite thing to do was to make a bird's nest out of the potatoes and gravy.

They seemed to taste even better this way.

When the girls scooped out the mound of potatoes onto their plates, they made a crater in the middle of their mound, and filled it with gravy. That's what they called a bird's nest.

Dinner was over, dishes were done, and the car was packed with suitcases and goodies. Grandma always had mouth-watering goodies to send home with the girls.

Katy Sunbeam and Cathy scoured the house, checking for anything they might have left behind. They hopped in the ol' brown truck while their heads were filled with treasured memories like pages from a diary.

The ol' brown truck bumped along the gravel road as it did just a short week ago when leaving the maple tree. Grandpa sang to the radio which helped to drown out the noise of the plastic wrap being opened in the back seat. Katy and Cathy couldn't wait to sink their teeth into their grandma's cookies. Oh, they were so good!

Katy's mouth was full of cookies, but she managed to blurt out, "I spy" when she spotted her mom's car under the maple tree. Kisses and hugs were once again exchanged under that ol' maple tree.

As Katy and Cathy pulled away from the ol' maple tree, they looked out the back window waving and blowing kisses to the ol' brown truck as it headed down the road in the opposite direction.

Printed in the United States
By Bookmasters